What's Left of the Flag

by Jimmy Murphy

SAMUELFRENCH-LONDON.CO.UK
SAMUELFRENCH.COM

Copyright © 2014 by Jimmy Murphy
All Rights Reserved

WHAT'S LEFT OF THE FLAG is fully protected under the copyright laws of the British Commonwealth, including Canada, the United States of America, and all other countries of the Copyright Union. All rights, including professional and amateur stage productions, recitation, lecturing, public reading, motion picture, radio broadcasting, television and the rights of translation into foreign languages are strictly reserved.

ISBN 978-0-573-11485-4

www.samuelfrench-london.co.uk

www.samuelfrench.com

For Amateur Production Enquiries

United Kingdom and World Excluding North America
plays@SamuelFrench-London.co.uk
020 7255 4302/01

United States and Canada
info@SamuelFrench.com
1-866-598-8449

Each title is subject to availability from Samuel French, depending upon country of performance.

CAUTION: Professional and amateur producers are hereby warned that WHAT'S LEFT OF THE FLAG is subject to a licensing fee. Publication of this play does not imply availability for performance. Both amateurs and professionals considering a production are strongly advised to apply to the appropriate agent before starting rehearsals, advertising, or booking a theatre. A licensing fee must be paid whether the title is presented for charity or gain and whether or not admission is charged.

The professional rights in this play are controlled by Curtis Brown, Haymarket House, 28-29 Haymarket, London SW1Y 4SP.

No one shall make any changes in this title for the purpose of production. No part of this book may be reproduced, stored in a retrieval system, or transmitted in any form, by any means, now known or yet to be invented, including mechanical, electronic, photocopying, recording, videotaping, or otherwise, without the prior written permission of the publisher. No one shall upload this title, or part of this title, to any social media websites.

The right of Jimmy Murphy to be identified as author of this work has been asserted by him in accordance with Section 77 of the Copyright, Designs and Patents Act 1988

JACOB *laughs aloud to himself.*

YOSSI. I'm going to file a report on this too.

JACOB. Good, good. Oh and don't forget the bit in about the swastika badges and the gas ovens. I liked that bit.

YOSSI *looks at him.* **JACOB** *throws the holdall over his shoulder. and heads to the door.*

I'll get the car started and will wait two minutes then leave. After that…you're on your own.

He stops, turns and looks back.

But believe this Yossi Amichai, if you think I'm crazy, then you really don't want to meet who they send out to track you down.

A look of fear on **YOSSI**'s *face.*

So be a good boy, huh, and torch the fucking place.

JACOB *exits.* **YOSSI** *stands looking after him. He picks up the matches, hesitates then strikes one and tosses it on to the floor. Sudden blackout as we hear the whoosh of flames starting up.*

THE END

What's Left of the Flag was first produced by Theatre Upstairs, Dublin on April 21st 2010. It was nominated for Best New Play in the Irish Times Theatre Awards 2011.

Cast

Jacob   Gerard Byrne

Yossi   Séan Flannagan

Director   Charlie Bonner

Stage Manager   Ryan McGeough

For Karl Shiels, le grá

A recently disused travel agents office in the city. Business debris is scattered around; PCs, phones, brochures, destination posters pinned to the wall. Two sleeping bags lie on the floor, on a desk bottled water, kettle, cups etc.

An iPod is playing a contemporary Israeli pop song in the background. **YOSSI** *is singing along to the song as he sits shuffling cards before dealing some out.*

YOSSI. 3 of... *(hesitates)* ... clubs.

He turns a card over to check then smiles.

Yes.

He thinks for a moment then calls out again.

7 of hearts, 9 of... diamonds, Jack of spades.

He turns 3 cards over in quick succession.

Shit, the Jack's before the 7. Concentrate. Yossi, concentrate Five of –

A door closing down stairs interrupts him. He goes to the door and stands, back against the wall and waits. When he hears three sharp raps on the door he opens it and returns to the cards.

JACOB *enters, wearing a baseball cap and carrying a large holdall and a bag of groceries from Tesco's, he looks to the iPod and barks.*

JACOB. What is this?

YOSSI *resists the urge to patronize.*

YOSSI. Music.

JACOB *puts the holdall out of the way and drops the groceries on the table.*

JACOB. Maybe you'd like to hang a flag out the window too?

YOSSI. It wasn't *that* loud.

JACOB. Or perhaps we'll put on a couple of yarmulkes and dance the Temani outside on the street?

YOSSI. Jesus Jacob… we're three floors up. In an abandoned building.

JACOB. Just turn it off and give me a hand with this.

> **YOSSI** *lowers the volume on the iPod.* **JACOB** *looks at him.*

I said off.

> **YOSSI** *takes a beat then turns the iPod off.*

YOSSI. Happy now?

> **JACOB** *patronizes him in Hebrew.*

JACOB. Toda raba. *thank you very much*

> **YOSSI** *is equally patronizing and mocks a bow.*

YOSSI. Be'vakasha. (*you're welcome*)

> *They stare at each other briefly then* **JACOB** *takes his jacket and cap off.*

One hour you said. You've been gone almost three. I needed something to relieve the boredom.

> **JACOB** *gives* **YOSSI** *a look.*

JACOB. Boredom…?

> *Then takes a file from the holdall and reads it.*

YOSSI. I was about to start talking to the walls.

JACOB. His first assignment and he gets bored. What have they sent me?

> **YOSSI** *goes through the groceries; milk, bread, cheese, tomatoes and a UK tabloid.*

YOSSI. Don't say you're not either.

JACOB. Twenty one years a katsa and not as much as one minute's been boring.

YOSSI. It's ok for you, you've been out a couple of times. Met with people.

JACOB. People! Schmohawk's at the embassy you mean. Crazy Irish Jews with *(Oirish accent) information of national importance.*

YOSSI *looks at the groceries and shakes his head.*

YOSSI. Is this it?

JACOB. There is a problem?

YOSSI. This is all the Sayanim bought for us?

JACOB. It's food, you should be grateful.

JACOB *closes the file and look at* **YOSSI** *before people.*

Read this.

YOSSI *takes the file.*

YOSSI. What is it?

JACOB. New intel.

YOSSI. You're kidding me?

JACOB. It came in this morning.

YOSSI. This morning! We got new intel yesterday.

JACOB. So someone wants to impress us with new information, big deal. Make his day and read the damn stuff, ok?

YOSSI *tosses the file aside.*

YOSSI. Later.

JACOB *looks at* **YOSSI** *then to the file, he seems concerned at something.* **YOSSI** *laughs to himself as he puts the groceries away.*

JACOB. Want to share the joke?

YOSSI. It's just that, well…you know. *Irish sayanims.*

This pisses **JACOB** *off.*

JACOB. There are sayanims all over the world.

YOSSI. I know I just meant –

JACOB. Everywhere! Jews willing to pass on information, do a favour for no other reason than to serve Israel.

JACOB *takes up the tabloid and flicks through it.*

YOSSI. Serve Israel, how about serving us? Cheese, bread ... tomatoes, what does he think we are? Mice?

JACOB. What do you care? You said you weren't hungry after last night's meal.

YOSSI *recoils at the mention of the meal.*

YOSSI. Ugh! Don't remind me. You almost killed me.

JACOB, *taken aback, puts the paper down.*

JACOB. Me? Me!

YOSSI. Yes you. You brought the shit back.

JACOB. I didn't cook it, did I?

YOSSI *is still baffled by the food.*

YOSSI. *Fish and chips.* What was that Jacob, huh, what the hell was that? I wouldn't give it to a dog.

JACOB. You think yours was bad? You should have tried my delicacy the "*battered burger*". They fry fucking... donkey meat or something, coat it in some shit then fry it all over again.

YOSSI. You went out to buy Italian food for our supper.

JACOB. They were Italians!

YOSSI. Harah! *(shit)*

JACOB. A whole fucking family of them. Standing there behind the counter like little gnomes. And up on the menu, you think there was any pasta, lasagna, pizza even? *Oi va'avoi li! (oh my god)* Not even garlic bread. What a fucking country.

YOSSI. Can you imagine what the Chinese food is like here?

JACOB. Donkey fucking stew or something.

They share a laugh as YOSSI *goes back to the cards while* JACOB *flicks through the newspaper in growing frustration.*

JACOB. Jesus...!

YOSSI. What?

JACOB. The Irish. They're so... so. *(finds the word)* English!

YOSSI laughs a little.

YOSSI. English...

JACOB. TV shows, football teams, newspapers. Everything about them. They get their freedom years ago and this is what they do with it?

JACOB helps himself to an apple.

It's wasted on some people, you know that?

YOSSI. Freedom?

JACOB. Look at us... just over sixty years old and one of the toughest countries in the world. Could take this shit hole over in one hour.

JACOB is enjoying YOSSI's boasting.

YOSSI. That long?

JACOB. You're right! 20 minutes, max, the whole damn country, north and south.

JACOB helps himself to an apple as YOSSI takes up the paper and looks through it.

You know they didn't fight the Nazis?

YOSSI. Like 20,000 drunken, potato eaters would have made a difference.

JACOB. In fact, and you won't believe this, their Prime Minister, ok?, their prime minister delivered his *condolences* to the German embassy when Hitler died. Can you believe that, huh, his fucking condolences!

YOSSI. So he had good manners, a good thing my mother always told me.

JACOB. I'll tell you one thing, if England was Israel's neighbour and had done all those things to us?

In mock horror.

Are you crazy? Are you fucking crazy! A barren wasteland it would be today, a desert.

YOSSI *tosses the paper aside, gets up and paces the room for a moment.*

YOSSI. Christ. I think today will never end.

JACOB. Stop moaning, you're like a little girl sometimes.

YOSSI. 2 days I've been stuck up here Jacob.

JACOB. 2 days. 2 days is nothing. 7 days I spent living in the back of a van one time. With 3 other katsas. 7 days!

YOSSI. I feel like my head's about to burst.

JACOB *shakes his head.*

JACOB. 6 weeks out of the academy and he forgets his training.

YOSSI. Training. I didn't spend 2 years training for this.

JACOB. Oh? And what did you train for then?

YOSSI. Not to be stuck up in some shit hole in Dublin, that's for sure.

JACOB. It's not a shit hole.

YOSSI. Are you crazy? Look at the state of this place Jacob. And sleeping on a floor?

JACOB. There are worse than this Yossi… you'll see. The day will come when you'll say *"oi, oi, oi that wonderful place in Dublin, now that was comfort, hey Jacob?"*

YOSSI *gets up, goes the window and tugs the curtain back slightly.*

YOSSI. Supposed to be the best available place overlooking the route. *Harah!*

JACOB. Jesus, put the music back on Yossi. You're giving me a headache.

YOSSI *returns to his seat.*

YOSSI. I'm sure there were better places than this, that's all I'm saying.

JACOB. An empty building with a perfect view of the podium, who cares what it's like inside?

YOSSI. *(beat)* And to take out, who, huh?

    JACOB *gives him a look.*

JACOB. Excuse me?

    YOSSI *takes up a photo and waves it at* JACOB.

YOSSI. A nobody.

    JACOB *is more shocked than angered.*

JACOB. A nobody?

YOSSI. Small fry. It's the big fish I want Jacob, the one's at the top. That's why I joined.

JACOB. Ibtisam Farsakh is small fry?

    YOSSI *hesitates.*

YOSSI. In my consideration… yes.

    JACOB *snatches a photo from the file.*

JACOB. Shootings in Gilo and Jericho –

YOSSI. – shootings

JACOB. – one which injured an army officer –

YOSSI. Injured.

JACOB. – a another attack on a bus on the Jericho bypass –

YOSSI. that failed

    JACOB *raises his voice.*

JACOB. – supplied weapons to the Tanzim, hid wanted men, dispatched a suicide bomber –

YOSSI. the bomber was shot

JACOB. You want me to go on Yossi, you want me to go on?

YOSSI. Farsakh hasn't been active for 7 years Jacob. Does that not mean anything?

    JACOB *tosses the photo at* YOSSI*'s chest, it falls to the ground.*

JACOB. 7 years or 700, it doesn't matter. They're an enemy of Israel. *(half under* YOSSI*'s breath)*

YOSSI. The whole damn world is according to Israel.

    JACOB *glares at him and spits the words out.*

JACOB. And don't you ever forget it.

A beat, **YOSSI** *looks at* **JACOB**.

They'd love to see us all dead. Everyone of them. And now this *coos. (cunt) (picks up the photo)* Thinks the Irish can save it? And the Irish? They think they can shelter someone with Israeli blood on their hands? Is the whole fucking world crazy?

JACOB *looks at the photo.*

Over my dead body.

YOSSI *cannot hold his tongue.*

YOSSI. They're not the only ones with blood on their hands, you know.

JACOB *looks at him, not sure what he's just heard.*

JACOB. Excuse me?

YOSSI *realises he's gone too far, he backs down.*

YOSSI. Nothing. Forget about it.

YOSSI *goes back to reading the paper.*

JACOB. The only blood we have on our hands is from the wounds we receive defending ourselves.

YOSSI. Shit.

JACOB *is more angered than shocked.*

JACOB. What did you just say?

YOSSI *pauses but is unable to hold his tongue. He gets up.*

YOSSI. Back in Gaza. There was this university we were sent in to "sweep up" after some gun fire from the rooftop. I was making my way along a corridor when something caught my eye on the wall. A large Israeli flag was painted on it. *(beat)* At least that's what I thought it was until I got up closer. The star of David was made from rifles and the two blue stripes… two lines of barbed wire.

JACOB. Fucking animals.

YOSSI. I couldn't stop looking at it Jacob, can't stop thinking about it. Still can't. I mean, when all this ends, if it all ends, is that what's left of the flag?

JACOB takes a beat, he stares at YOSSI then speaks.

JACOB. You have a loose tongue Yossi Amichai. Be careful you don't trip over it some day.

Realising he's gone a little too far YOSSI backtracks.

YOSSI. I'm sorry. It's here, this room. The air, it stinks.

JACOB takes a beat.

JACOB. Ze be'seder. (*it's ok*)

JACOB puts the holdall on the table.

This is what delayed me this morning. Dumb schmohawk at the embassy couldn't find the diplomatic bag.

YOSSI. You're kidding me?

JACOB. 30 minutes running around the place... you should have seen him. Crying he was.

YOSSI. No...?

JACOB. My hand to God. Like a little baby. Terrified I'd report him and he'd lose his job.

YOSSI laughs.

And where was it... huh? Where did he leave it? In his car.

YOSSI. Jesus!

JACOB. Can you believe that, he left it in his trunk after he picked it up at the airport last night.

JACOB takes out a couple of fake passports from the holdall. He opens one and looks at the picture.

Lavrentis Dianellos...

YOSSI. Hmm?

JACOB. I didn't know you spoke Greek.

JACOB tosses the passport to YOSSI, *he catches it and looks through it.*

You're an Athenian dentist going back.

JACOB looks through the other passport.

Ani lo ma'amin! (*I don't believe it*)

YOSSI. Something wrong?

JACOB. I'll give you one guess…

A smile breaks out on YOSSI*'s face.*

YOSSI. Canadian?

JACOB. Mossad and the Canadians. Always with the Canadians.

He tosses the passport aside. YOSSI *looks at it and laughs.*

YOSSI. Kirk Taylor.

JACOB. I sound like a… 70's porn star.

JACOB tosses a wad of euros on the table, YOSSI *counts them out.*

YOSSI. There's 300 here.

JACOB. So?

YOSSI. They expecting us to hang around?

JACOB. If the office want to throw money around what do you care? Buy your little girly something nice at the airport this evening if you want.

YOSSI. Maybe I will.

JACOB. Meeting her tonight?

YOSSI looks at him, shrugs his shoulder.

YOSSI. Perhaps…

JACOB laughs.

JACOB. Perhaps. Perhaps, he says.

A smile breaks out on YOSSI*'s face.*

What's her name...? Monica! Yes, sweet little Monica with the green eyes, the long brown hair... and those wonderful tits.

YOSSI. You're a dirty old man, Jacob, do you know that?

JACOB laughs as **YOSSI** *goes back to counting the cards.*

Ace of diamonds, 4 of spades...

JACOB starts to watch **YOSSI**. **YOSSI** *turns two cards over.*

King of hearts... 2 of clubs... 8 of spades.

JACOB. Yossi...

Turning more cards over.

YOSSI. Hmm...?

JACOB. Can I ask you one thing?

YOSSI. Sure

JACOB. What's with the cards all the time?

YOSSI. The cards...?

JACOB. Every time I look at you you're sitting down calling out cards to yourself.

YOSSI laughs a little.

YOSSI. I'm counting.

JACOB. Counting?

YOSSI. Teaching myself to count cards.

JACOB. 1, 2, 3, 4. There, it's easy.

YOSSI. It's a little more complicated than that.

JACOB. Oh?

YOSSI. Black Jack.

JACOB. The card game?

YOSSI. Casinos; Monaco, Venice, London. Where I'm going to be posted when I get back.

JACOB. *(impressed)* Nice.

YOSSI. Turn rich Arabs, or not so rich. It's a good cover.

JACOB. Clever that. Not like my first cover.

JACOB *pulls up a chair beside* YOSSI.

Set up as a publisher in Zurich. Froze the *beitsim (balls)* off myself there. A card player, now that's good, night life, money... women.

YOSSI *looks at* JACOB*'s wedding ring finger,* JACOB *moves his hand away.*

YOSSI. Wanna try me out?

JACOB. Huh?

YOSSI. Your half of the three hundred.

JACOB. *Harah!*

YOSSI. Come on, pull up a chair, I'll test my skills on you.

JACOB *goes to the window and pulls the curtain back as the room is awash with sunlight.*

JACOB. Some other time. I may teach you a thing or two.

He looks out the window with the binoculars.

People are starting to gather.

YOSSI. Let me see...

YOSSI *gets up,* JACOB *passes him the binoculars.*

JACOB. *Boycott Israel.* Fucking assholes. Where's a suicide bomber when you need one?

YOSSI. That's not funny.

JACOB *looks at him.*

JACOB. Who's joking? If they can do it, why can't we?

YOSSI *hands* JACOB *the binoculars back.*

What time is it now?

YOSSI *looks at the watch on* JACOB*'s wrist,* JACOB *barks at him.*

It's stopped!

YOSSI *looks at his watch.*

YOSSI. 1:20. The protest starts at what, 1:30?

JACOB. Give or take a few minutes.

> JACOB *takes a beat.*

Right, we better get ready.

> JACOB *goes to the holdall and takes out a long range sniper rifle. he hands it to* YOSSI. YOSSI *stares at the rifle.*

Nervous?

YOSSI. No. Maybe a little –

JACOB. Excited?

YOSSI. I was going to say *concerned.*

> YOSSI *checks the scope, chamber etc.*

YOSSI. How long?

JACOB. What?

YOSSI. From here to the car.

> JACOB*'s reply is a little snippy.*

JACOB. Christ, 2, 3 minutes max! I've tested it a dozen times, ok!

YOSSI. Jesus Jacob, lighten up.

> JACOB *takes a beat, then smiles at* YOSSI.

JACOB. Sorry. Sometimes I get…tense before a job.

> *This surprises* YOSSI.

YOSSI. You do?

JACOB. You never expect anything to go wrong but…

> YOSSI *takes a beat, a sense of fear in his voice.*

YOSSI. But sometimes it does?

> JACOB *looks at him for a moment, then, hiding his concern.*

JACOB. How about you make some coffee and I check the rifle, huh?

> YOSSI *hands* JACOB *the rifle then goes to the kettle.*

And no so strong this time, Jesus! Fucking tar you cooked up this morning. I thought I was back in a Turkish prison.

YOSSI *gives him a look.*

I'll tell you about it some other time.

YOSSI *plugs the kettle in then puts the iPod on, low. An old Israeli pop song plays.* **JACOB** *gives him a look, then smiles as he puts a silencer on the rifle.*

YOSSI. Hungry?

JACOB. Perhaps a sandwich, we won't get to eat for a while.

YOSSI *spoons some coffee into a cafetiere and boils a kettle as the music plays in the background. Throughout the following he prepares some cheese and tomato sandwiches.*

YOSSI. So tell me Jacob. You married?

JACOB *freezes for a second.*

JACOB. No. *(pauses)* Well. I was.

YOSSI. Hmm…got caught with a lover?

JACOB. *(beat)* No.

YOSSI. Let me guess, the hours, away from home too much? You hear it so much at the academy. Marriage and Mossad, it's either one or the other.

JACOB's *mood has saddened during this,* **YOSSI** *doesn't notice until a silence hangs.*

Is there something wrong?

JACOB *pauses briefly.*

JACOB. Ten years ago. My wife and son were…killed in a suicide attack on a café in Tel Aviv.

The news leaves **YOSSI** *lost for words.*

YOSSI. Jacob. I'm… I'm–Ani mitzar. *(I'm so sorry)*

JACOB. What are you sorry for, you didn't do it.

YOSSI *turns the iPod off.*

They'd gone out to buy me a watch for my birthday. I was due back from Paris that morning.

He holds his arm up with the watch.

10:41, Tuesday 6th June…

YOSSI *goes to* **JACOB** *and grips his shoulder.*

YOSSI. I am… so sorry my friend.

He smiles at **YOSSI**, *slaps his face gently.*

JACOB. Kacha hachaim, hey? (*that's life*) *(to himself)* Kacha hachaim…

He puts the rifle against the wall and forces a sudden upbeat tone.

Never liked long shots.

YOSSI. Never?

JACOB. There's no rush in this, no thrill. In my day you got to look into their eyes, did the job in 2 seconds. Bang, bang. Bang, No… no hiding in an office waiting on the right moment. This shit, we have robots back in Israel, that can do this, robots.

YOSSI. Well I guess it ain't your day any more, is it old man?

JACOB *smiles as* **YOSSI** *pours boiling water into the cafetiere.*

JACOB. I guess not. New ways, methods… ideas. There's even talk that I may be recalled to Tel Aviv.

YOSSI *is a little surprised at this.*

YOSSI. Recalled?

JACOB. To instruct at the academy.

YOSSI. Ah. Instructor. That's great news Jacob.

JACOB. You think so?

YOSSI. To train the next generation of field agents? Of course. I mean, you're a legend.

JACOB. *(dismissively)* Legend…

YOSSI. The man who eliminated the famous Mahmoud Keshkesh?

JACOB *is a little surprised.*

JACOB. They still talk about that at the academy?

YOSSI. Talk about it? We studied the case reports.

A sore point. **JACOB** *hesitates.*

Didn't you study case reports in your time. Analyze operations, see what went wrong, how it could be avoided etc.

JACOB *smiles at this.*

JACOB. Keshkesh was no big deal.

YOSSI. Listen to him! He killed 9 soldiers, the best sniper the Palestinians ever had.

JACOB *pauses, he smiles as he recalls.*

JACOB. It took us months, but we finally tracked him down to a Milan hotel. After 3 days of trailing we decided to take him out on a bus. He's sitting at the back reading a paper, Mordechai drives along side on a motorcycle, I pull out my glock and fire 6 shots to the head. 3 hours later we're back in Tel Aviv, drinking cocktails and chasing women. That Yossi, that's how you operate.

YOSSI *takes a beat as he puts the coffee on the table.*

YOSSI. Mordechai?

JACOB. What?

YOSSI. Mordechai Yatom?

JACOB *looks at* **YOSSI** *for a few seconds.*

JACOB. That's right.

YOSSI *nods his head in silence. It pisses* **JACOB** *off.*

What's with the nodding?

YOSSI. Nothing.

JACOB. Don't fuck around with me, Yossi. I can read people like books.

YOSSI *is a little flippant.*

YOSSI. It's just, at the academy.

JACOB. You studied that operation too?
YOSSI. Every operation. You know that.
JACOB. Well...?
YOSSI. How he died. Or the way he died... it was. Odd.

    JACOB *pauses.*

JACOB. He was killed in action.
YOSSI. I didn't say he wasn't.
JACOB. So why bring his name up?
YOSSI. I didn't. You did.
JACOB. If you've something to say, then say it.

    YOSSI *puts the sandwiches on the desk.*

YOSSI. Please, Jacob you're ruining the lunch, sit down.

    A silence hangs.

JACOB. In our business the job is all, understand, all or nothing.
YOSSI. Please Jacob, eat your sandwich... hey?

    JACOB *pauses then takes a mouthful of coffee then spits it out.*

JACOB. Jesus, I told you not so strong!
YOSSI. I'll make some fresh stuff.

    YOSSI *gets up.*

JACOB. It's ok.
YOSSI. It's no bother, 2 minutes, I'll make a fresh pot.
JACOB. Christ do you ever listen! I said it's ok, alright?

    YOSSI *returns to his lunch. a silence hangs. a look of guilt on* **JACOB**.

    I'm eh... I'm sorry

    YOSSI *just nods his head.*

    My bark. It's worse than...

YOSSI. *Ze be'seder.*

    JACOB *drinks some coffee. He holds his cup up.*

JACOB. But you're coffee… it's still shit.

They both share a laugh.

YOSSI. I ask too many questions anyway.

JACOB. I don't know, in the Mossad that's not considered a fault.

Now come on… the new intel.

YOSSI *dismisses the suggestion as he eats.*

YOSSI. I had my commander driven mad at the academy. "Questions, always with the questions Yossi."

JACOB *gets up and stands by the window with his coffee looking out.*

JACOB. He was my best friend, Mordecai. We became katsas at the same time.

YOSSI *sits back and listens.*

A big, tough Jew from Hungary. In the Yom Kippur war he ambushed a Syrian patrol, killed everyone of them single handedly then drove their fucking tank back to his base!

He holds a silence then shakes his head as he recalls.

The mission was fool proof. We'd gone over and over it a hundred times; I'd wait across the street in a van, Mordichai'd pick the lock, run upstairs and plant the bomb in their apartment. When they returned I'd set it off from the van then drive us to the airport.

He sits, a pain in his voice.

Everyday, for 5 days we tracked them and every day the same; stop off in a small café, drink coffee for an hour or so, the same order, the same seats even.

YOSSI *breaks the silence.*

YOSSI. So what went wrong?

JACOB *hesitates, he shrugs his shoulders.*

JACOB. I don't know. They didn't stop for coffee that morning? All I do know is that just as Mordechai opened the door they pulled up outside.

YOSSI hesitates then.

YOSSI. Didn't he try and run?

JACOB ignores the question.

Or you. Didn't you…help? Distract them?

JACOB doesn't answer and stares out blankly.

Jacob…?

He bangs the desk with his fist.

JACOB. What could I do, huh? The job is all, that's what they drill in to you at the academy, from day one. *"Success of the mission is the only acceptable outcome."*

JACOB repeats to himself, quietly.

Success is the only acceptable outcome…

YOSSI breaks the silence.

YOSSI. I would have opened fire.

JACOB snaps at him.

JACOB. And jeopardize the mission?

YOSSI. It's a risk but…

JACOB. Idiot! The mission is all.

YOSSI. Even if it means –

JACOB. All the time!

YOSSI. I disagree.

JACOB roars leaving a silence in his wake.

JACOB. All the fucking time!

The silence hangs.

YOSSI. So you… you drove off?

JACOB. What else, left flowers outside the building. "*Dear Mordechai, sadly missed by Jacob and all the boys in the Mossad*"

JACOB *takes a beat, then, coldly.*

You don't have to pretend. I know what they say at the academy, heard the rumours. That he detonated his bomb before they could kill him and that...

He stops. **YOSSI** *finishes the sentence.*

YOSSI. That he was Israel's only suicide bomber.

JACOB *nods his head.*

And was he?

JACOB *is furious as this, he flings his cup against the wall and shouts.*

JACOB. What was he to do, huh? Let them capture him alive? Torture him until he spoke and then kill him?

YOSSI *stays silent and watches* **JACOB** *load the rifle with a bullet.*

Never, never in the history of the Mossad has a katsa ever been captured and I wasn't going to let Mordechai be the first.

This surprises **YOSSI.**

YOSSI. You weren't?

YOSSI *stares at him, the only sound is of* **JACOB**'*s heavy breathing as he calms down.*

What do you mean, "*you weren't*" Jacob?

The silence is interrupted by a distant sound of a crowd cheering. **JACOB** *goes to the window and opens it. The sound from the street below enters the room.*

JACOB. The speeches have started. It will be time soon.

YOSSI *looks suspiciously at* **JACOB.**

Well, what are you waiting for? Get ready.

> YOSSI *takes up the rifle, checks it then goes to the window.*

It's to your requirements?

> YOSSI *is suddenly cold and distant with* JACOB.

YOSSI. Perfect.

> *As* YOSSI *checks the range through the scope.*

JACOB. And the distance?

YOSSI. No problem.

JACOB. You have a good view of the podium?

YOSSI. I said no problem.

> *They look at each other until a louder cheer goes up from the crowd and the sound of someone speaking from a megaphone.*

JACOB. The target's arrived.

> YOSSI *takes up his position.* JACOB *stands behind, observing with the binoculars.*

You see Farsakh? Back of the platform, red coat... scarf.

> YOSSI *looks through the scope.*

YOSSI. I have her.

JACOB. Clear shot?

YOSSI. One moment...there is someone in the way.

> YOSSI *pauses as he focuses in.*

Clear.

JACOB. She is next to speak. Once she has started you may fire when ready.

> *Suddenly* YOSSI *recoils. He jumps back, dropping the rifle to the floor.*

YOSSI. Jesus!

> JACOB *barks an order.*

JACOB. Back in position. Now!

YOSSI. Jesus Christ Jacob…can't you see?

JACOB. I said, back in to position.

YOSSI takes a beat.

YOSSI. She's pregnant!

JACOB holds his look, then, coldly.

JACOB. So, we get two for the price of one. What do you care?

YOSSI is shocked.

YOSSI. Jacob…?

JACOB. You want to know when and where the *coos* (*cunt*) conceived?

I can tell you if you like.

YOSSI. I… I wasn't told this.

JACOB's reply is smart assed.

JACOB. The new intel. You mean you never got to read it?

YOSSI glances over at the file.

YOSSI. This is wrong, Jacob…

JACOB. You have your orders Yossi.

YOSSI. I can't shoot a pregnant woman.

JACOB. Can't or won't?

YOSSI hesitates.

YOSSI. We need to call someone.

JACOB. What's wrong with you? You're file said you were ruthless in Gaza. Excelled yourself in worse situations.

YOSSI. I will not repeat the evils of Gaza, Jacob, never.

JACOB takes a beat.

JACOB. Evils of Gaza? We haven't got a conscience now, have we?

YOSSI. Hasn't everyone? Or are Jews different?

JACOB. To be a good Jew you need a good conscience, to be a good Israeli you need a good memory. What you need to work out Yossi is which one you are.

YOSSI. I thought I could be both.

JACOB. The Mossad doesn't kill for Judaism... it kills for Israel and Israel only.

YOSSI. I left the army and it's butchers because of that shit. And now here, it's the same here?

JACOB. Butchers?

YOSSI. Have you any idea what we did in there?

JACOB. We did well to slip that little analysis through the physiological test at the academy, didn't we?

This angers **YOSSI.**

YOSSI. I was honest at the Academy.

JACOB. *Harah!*

YOSSI. Told them how I felt about shooting–

JACOB. *(shouts)* – terrorists!

YOSSI. Terrorists? Old men, women... children?

JACOB. The old men, more than likely, used to be terrorists, the women, producers of terrorists and the children would undoubtedly have grown up to be terrorists. You ask me Gaza was a superb exercise in eliminating the past, present and future murdering scum.

YOSSI *stares at him in silence then speaks slowly and quietly.*

YOSSI. Whenever I hear a Jew speak like that, I can't help but wonder how a little badge with a swastika on it wouldn't look so out of place on their lapel.

JACOB *slaps* **YOSSI** *hard on the face.* **YOSSI** *shouts back.*

The only difference between them and us is that we haven't got the balls to use gas chambers...

JACOB *raises his hand again but* **YOSSI** *grabs it,* **JACOB** *struggles to break free but* **YOSSI** *is too strong, eventually he let's* **JACOB**'*s wrist go.*

That one was for free Jacob. But try it again and I'll rip your fucking head off and piss in the hole.

They stare at each other then **YOSSI** *turns to compose himself as* **JACOB** *goes to the holdall.*

JACOB. If you wanted a nice job Yossi... you should have gone selling flowers to the tourists in Haifa.

JACOB *takes out a pistol, cocks it and points it at* **YOSSI**.

Now for the last time...back into position.

YOSSI *turns and sees the gun.*

YOSSI. What the hell are you doing?

JACOB. Farsakh's speech will last six minutes. You've already wasted three.

YOSSI. Are you crazy?

JACOB *speaks coldly to* **YOSSI**.

JACOB. Trust me Yossi, you wouldn't like to find out.

YOSSI. I won't do it Jacob.

JACOB. And sacrifice yourself for a Palestinian *coos*?

There is real fear growing in **YOSSI**'*s voice as the sound of the speaker fills the room.*

YOSSI. Jacob, please. Put the gun down.

JACOB. Don't think I won't shoot...my hand to God Yossi, I will pull the trigger.

YOSSI. Please. I beg of you. Don't make me do this.

JACOB. The choice is yours; a dead Jew or a dead Palestinian...

YOSSI *gestures to the rifle.*

YOSSI. You. You do it...

JACOB. You're the fucking sniper, not me.

YOSSI. This is what happened to Mordechai, isn't it?

JACOB. *(shouts)* Fuck Mordechai!

YOSSI. You detonated the bomb. You made him run in with it then set it off?

YOSSI *back tracks around the room with* **JACOB** *following him, the gun aimed at* **YOSSI**'*s head.*

JACOB. I *helped* him complete our mission, if that's what you mean.

JACOB puts the guns to YOSSI's head.

Just as I will help you complete this one too.

(JACOB cocks the pistol) Ten...nine.

YOSSI. Please Jacob no...

JACOB. Eight. Seven.

Tears in YOSSI's voice.

YOSSI. You can't do this...

JACOB. Six, five, four.

YOSSI. Jacob this is murder.

JACOB. Three, two. Goodbye Yossi.

YOSSI screams.

YOSSI. Ok, ok!

YOSSI grabs the rifle, takes aim then fires. The speaker stops, brief silence then the sound of panic from the streets below. JACOB looks through the binoculars.

JACOB. A kill.

JACOB closes the window and draws the curtains back.

Good.

There are tears in YOSSI's voice.

YOSSI. You bastard. You sick, fucking bastard.

JACOB places the rifle and pistol in the holdall.

JACOB. Cry later, on the plane. For now, get the gasoline.

YOSSI sits crying with his head in his hands, JACOB shouts.

Yossi! The gasoline.

YOSSI ignores him so JACOB fetches a plastic container, takes the lid off and empties petrol around the place. That done he throws the holdall over his shoulder.

YOSSI. Jacob...?

JACOB *ignores him and heads to the door.* **YOSSI** *shouts.*

Jacob!

JACOB *stops and turns.*

JACOB. What?

YOSSI. Would you have...?

JACOB. Shot you?

YOSSI *nods.* **JACOB** *pauses briefly.*

You did your duty, the question is hypothetical, irrelevant.

YOSSI *grabs* **JACOB** *by the collar.*

YOSSI. Would you have shot me!

JACOB *pushes* **YOSSI** *away, takes a beat.*

JACOB. I never shoot Jews.

The reply leaves **YOSSI** *stunned. He kicks a chair across the room and screams.*

YOSSI. Bastard...!

JACOB *gives* **YOSSI** *a moment.*

JACOB. You have eliminated an enemy of Israel. Know what that makes you now? Where it places you in the Mossad?

YOSSI. To hell with you and the Mossad.

JACOB*'s tone lightens.*

JACOB. Perhaps your first kill for the office was a little unpleasant. It's like that sometimes. Next month, who knows, maybe you'll hunt down a nuclear scientist in Holland, an arms dealer in Prague. Either way, you'll move on, we all do. Now get your stuff.

JACOB *slaps him on the back.*

YOSSI. Azov oti! (*leave me alone*) I'm not going with you.

JACOB. And what? You'll stay here, spend the rest of your days in an Irish jail counting cards to yourself?

www.ingramcontent.com/pod-product-compliance
Lightning Source LLC
Chambersburg PA
CBHW070455050426
42450CB00012B/3290